Who Was Louis Armstrong?

Colin Foley

ROSEN
COMMON CORE
READERS

Rosen Classroom™

New York

Published in 2014 by The Rosen Publishing Group, Inc.
29 East 21st Street, New York, NY 10010

Book Design: Katelyn Londino

Photo Credits: Cover David Redfern/Redferns/Getty Images; p. 5 New York Daily News Archive/Getty Images; p. 7 Underwood Archives/Getty Images; p. 9 tHaNtHiMa LiM/Shutterstock.com; p. 11 en.wikipedia.org/wiki/File:Riverboats_at_Memphis.jpg/Wikipedia.org; p. 13 Frank Driggs Collection/Archive Photos/Getty Images; p. 15 (Carnegie Hall) Gabriel Hackett/Hulton Archive/Getty Images; p. 15 (inset) Gilles Petard/Redferns/Getty Images; p. 17 Hulton Archive/Archive Photos/Getty Images; p. 19 Express Newpapers/Hulton Archive/Getty Images; p. 21 Michael Ochs Archives/Getty Images.

ISBN: 978-1-4777-2278-7
6-pack ISBN: 978-1-4777-2279-4

Manufactured in the United States of America

CPSIA Compliance Information: Batch #CS13RC: For further information contact Rosen Publishing, New York, New York at 1-800-237-9932.

Contents

Who Was He?

Jazz is a kind of music that's special because it was born in the United States. Jazz **musicians** use many different **rhythms** and often make up parts as they play. This is called improvisation. Louis Armstrong is one of the founders of jazz. He made it common to play long **solos** in jazz songs. People called him "Satchmo" and "Pops."

Louis Armstrong was a very talented singer, actor, and trumpet player. This is Louis and his trumpet.

Early Life

Louis was born on August 4, 1901, in New Orleans, Louisiana. He liked to be called "Louie." He grew up in a scary neighborhood. People who lived there were very poor. Many gangs fought there. By age 7, Louis had to make money for his family. He sang on street corners for money. He entered into the world of music early in his life.

New Orleans has been a great center for jazz music since the early 1900s.

HOLMES
KRESS
PALACE
HANAN & SON

When he was young, Louis was sent to live in a home for boys who got in trouble. He took his first music classes there. When he left the home, he started to play music with other bands around New Orleans. Then, he studied music with Joe Oliver. Joe was one of the best trumpet players in New Orleans.

Trumpets are one of the key instruments in jazz music.

Louis still had to make money for his family. He got a job playing music on a **steamboat** that went up and down the Mississippi River. There, he learned how to play different kinds of music. He learned how to read music, too. He had become a real musician.

Steamboats were easy ways to get people and things from place to place along the river.

PACKET CO.

Chicago

Joe Oliver, Louis's teacher, asked him to come to Chicago to play in his jazz band. Louis also began traveling around the country, playing music. Louis led a band of his own, called the Hot Five. The band recorded their songs so more people could listen to them.

In Chicago, Louis started "scat singing." That's when you sing using made-up words. Scat singing is still popular in jazz music.

The Greatest

New York City was home to the world's greatest jazz musicians. Louis moved there in 1929, and many bands wanted him to join them. He recorded songs with the most famous people in the world of jazz, such as Ella Fitzgerald and Duke Ellington. He played in the most famous music halls—even Carnegie Hall!

Since 1891, Carnegie Hall has been one of the most famous music halls in the world.

Ella Fitzgerald and Louis Armstrong

Acting

Louis Armstrong wasn't just a good musician. He could act, too. He acted on Broadway, which is a part of New York City with many important **theaters**. He also acted in movies, such as *Pennies from Heaven* and *Hello, Dolly!* He appeared in over 20 movies in his lifetime!

Louis acted with a very famous actress named Barbra Streisand in *Hello, Dolly!*

The Jazz Ambassador

Louis Armstrong was called "Ambassador Satch." An ambassador is someone sent to other countries to give messages or make peace. Louis Armstrong brought the message of jazz to the rest of the world. He traveled to many places, such as France, Germany, Italy, and many African countries.

Louis Armstrong even traveled to Egypt to play his music!

Louis Armstrong played music for the rest of his life. Even when he was sick, he played music whenever he could. A few days before he died, he was still getting ready for shows. Louis died on July 6, 1971. Even after his death, his music lived on.

People knew Louis Armstrong because of his music and also because of his big smile!

The Talents of Louis Armstrong

Glossary

musician (myoo-ZIH-shuhn) A person who plays, sings, or writes music.

rhythm (RIH-thuhm) Ordered patterns of beats or sounds in a song.

solo (SOH-loh) A part in a song played by one person.

steamboat (STEEM-boht) A boat that runs on steam power.

theater (THEE-uh-tuhr) A building where plays and movies are shown.

Index